Riccardo L. Harris

Misery to

Motivation

B.Global Publishing

Misery to Motivation
By Riccardo L. Harris

ISBN: 9780615692272

Copyright © 2012 B.global Publishing

All Rights Reserved. No part of this publication may be reproduced in any form or by any means, without written permission from the publisher.

B.Global Publishing
6341 Eilerts
Wichita, KS 67218

Printed in the United States of America

Misery to Motivation
By Riccardo L. Harris

Rozie, Raven and Rachel, we have come this far by faith. Let's continue to fight...
For Robert

Contents

Part I-Misery

1. That Fateful Day — 6
2. My Son Robert — 16
3. Failing as a Father — 25
4. God Why? — 31
5. Forgiveness — 41

Part II-Motivation

6. The Character Challenge — 52

Respect   *54*

Responsibility   *59*

Resilience   *61*

7. A Dream Deferred — 72
8. Dealing with Frustration — 84
9. Dealing with the Scars — 90

Conclusion — 95

Misery to Motivation
By Riccardo L. Harris

Misery

Chapter 1
That Fateful Day

January 5, 2008 was a strange winter day. It was unseasonably warm outside, 57 degrees. At least an inch of snow had been on the ground for the previous two weeks. The snow was melting and everybody was excited because of the nice weather. Little did I know, this day would be filled with extreme excitement, tremendous hurt, and it would change my life forever.

It was basketball season and I was an assistant coach for the Southeast High School basketball team. On this day there would be a powerhouse showdown between the state's top high school basketball teams; East High School and Southeast High School. The game was held at Koch Arena on the campus of Wichita State University.

The game was one of the best basketball games I have ever seen. Southeast trailed by four points with about four seconds to go. Everybody in the arena thought the game was surely over. The Southeast point guard took the in-bound pass and dribbled the length of the court. He pulled up and shot a three-pointer. While in the air he was bumped by a player from East. The ball bounced around the rim and went through the net. The horn blew signaling the end of the game, but there was a foul called by the referee. The referee called a foul on the East player who bumped the point guard while in the act of shooting. The point guard goes to the line and shoots a foul shot and sends the game into overtime. Southeast ultimately wins the game after two overtimes.

    After the game, I was overwhelmed with emotion. I was so excited. I could not believe that our team had won the game. The other coaches and I went out to eat to celebrate the victory. When I was walking into the restaurant, my phone rang. It was one of the players from my team. I knew something was wrong because his voice was shaky and he was screaming. He said,

"Coach, Robert has been shot. You need to come to the hospital right away."

I hung up the phone in disbelief. I jumped in my car and drove to the hospital. I can remember praying and saying 'God, please let it be a minor injury…Let him be okay.'

When I arrived at the hospital, I parked across the street because the emergency room entrance had been blocked off by police crime tape. I jumped out of my car and ran. It seemed like I was running in slow motion. When I finally got to the hospital, I asked a police officer how my son was doing. He instructed me to go inside the hospital and be with my family.

My wife, Rosaland, and my daughters, Raven and Rachel, arrived at the hospital shortly after I did. When we saw each other we hugged. I asked what happened. They didn't know much information and I didn't have any information to share. The hospital staff had given us access to a quiet room so that we could have some privacy. I could not sit down. I kept pacing back and forth. Each time a doctor or nurse came near us, I was expecting to hear how Robert was doing. Finally after about four hours of waiting, the hospital staff and the police officers came out to tell us what happened. The doctor looked at me and said,

"Your son came in with 2 gunshot wounds, one in the arm, and the other in his neck. We tried our best to stop the bleeding. I'm sorry, we could not save him."

I have never felt so helpless in my life. The doctor told me my son was dead. I looked around the room and I saw the hurt and disbelief in my wife's eyes. One of my daughters said, "Daddy No."

My mother-in-law collapsed.

I felt like somebody had knocked the wind out of me. I thought I was having a bad dream.

My wife asked the doctors if we could see him. The police detective answered and said we could not see him because his body was considered to be a crime scene and they needed to do an autopsy and gather evidence from his body.

The last time I saw my son alive…was just before he left the house that afternoon. He stood next to me and said,

"Dad, I'm getting to be as tall as you".

I said,

"No son, you will never be as tall as me."

I hugged him around his neck and we laughed.

If I had known that was going to be the last time I hugged my son, I would have held on to him.

I finally had the opportunity to see my son's body after he had been prepared by the mortuary. The reality of the fact that my son was dead became very real at the moment I saw him.

On January 5, 2008 my life changed forever. My 19 year old son Robert Pierre Ridge was killed by a young man who felt he looked at him the wrong way.

Robert picked up some friends from the basketball game (The same basketball game where I experienced such great joy). He was driving to drop them off at their respective homes when he stopped at a stop light. Robert turned right at the light and pulled over to wait for some of his other friends who were trailing him in another car. While parked and waiting, a car pulled up next to Robert. The driver of the other vehicle pulled out a gun and started shooting. He fired four gunshots. Robert was hit twice; one bullet hit him in his elbow, and the other bullet hit him in the carotid artery on the left side of his neck.

The shooter had seen Robert and his friends at the stop light. Apparently, he felt like Robert or someone in the vehicle looked at him the wrong way.

Robert realized he had been shot and tried to drive himself to the hospital. He was one block away from the hospital. Robert backed up his car, and attempted to turn around and drive to the hospital, but the car got stuck on the curb. By this time, his friends in the car behind him arrived on the scene. Robert got out of the car and asked his friends to take him to the hospital. They put Robert in the car and drove him to the emergency room. Robert was bleeding profusely. The hospital personnel rushed out to the car and took Robert into the trauma room. They could not stop the bleeding. The bullet that hit Robert in the neck hit the carotid artery on his left side and traveled to the carotid artery on the right side. There was no way to save him. Robert died a short while after arriving at the hospital.

According to Wichita Police Sgt. Brian White,
"by the time I got here, his friends had pulled him out of the car and driven him to the hospital," White said. *"I went there. He could barely talk. His friends... his friends were, needless to say, very*

distraught." Gangbangers, even when one of their friends gets killed, act disrespectfully and turn away from cops, White said. But Ridge's friends were not gangbangers. They gave police clear, accurate descriptions of the shooter's car, which quickly led to an arrest." (Wichita Eagle newspaper)

    The perpetrator of this horrific crime was caught within 30 minutes thanks to the description given by Robert's friends and an eye witness.

    Robert Ridge was a victim of a senseless act of violence. He was not in a gang, nor did he associate himself with gang members.

    I knew that I could not allow my son's death to be in vain so I decided to do something. I decided to tell Robert's story to as many people who would listen. Hopefully people will learn that violence affects everybody. Robert was not involved in gangs or the gang lifestyle and violence found him. Gang violence not only affects those involved in gang activity; it affects an entire community.

    That day was filled with excitement, but it ended with extreme hurt and disbelief. The loss of my son Robert has brought misery to me and my family, but it has also motivated me to stand up and tell the story about Robert's life, his untimely death and to challenge people to be their very best.

Misery to Motivation
By Riccardo L. Harris

Waste
The tragic human toll of gang violence

He was 19 and had his whole life ahead of him. But because a gang thug didn't like the way he looked at him, Robert Ridge is dead, police say.
For a look.
What a waste. What an outrage.

Ridge, Robert Pierre, 19, former Spirit Aerosystems sheet metal employee, died Jan. 5, 2008. Service 1:30 p.m. Friday, St. Mark United Methodist Church, 1525 N. Lorraine. Survivors: parents, Riccardo and Rosaland Harris; brother, Adrian Hall; sisters, Adrianna and Simone Hall, Shabrell, Raven and Rachel Harris; grandparents, Cheniia Holloway, Cynthia Ridge-Henderson, Robert Ridge, James and Parice Armstrong, Billy Ray Harris. Entrusted to Jackson Mortuary.

Police say dirty look led to homicide

After son's death, dad has solemn mission

Chapter 2
My Son Robert

Youth offers the promise of happiness, but life offers the realities of grief.
                Nicholas Sparks, *The Rescue*

Misery to Motivation
By Riccardo L. Harris

Robert Pierre Ridge was born on March 1, 1988. He was 6 lbs. and 12 ounces. He grew up as an active little boy. My son Robert's smile could light up a room. He was a fun loving and mild mannered person. His mother describes him as "a loving and giving person who didn't allow anybody to mess with his family." Robert was funny too. He did not always allow everybody to see his funny side.

Robert was a great young man with many gifts and talents. He enjoyed working out at the gym, drawing and hanging out with his friends. Robert had an uncanny ability to make others laugh. He was a joy to be around. His quiet and silent strength affected everybody he had contact with.

Misery to Motivation
By Riccardo L. Harris

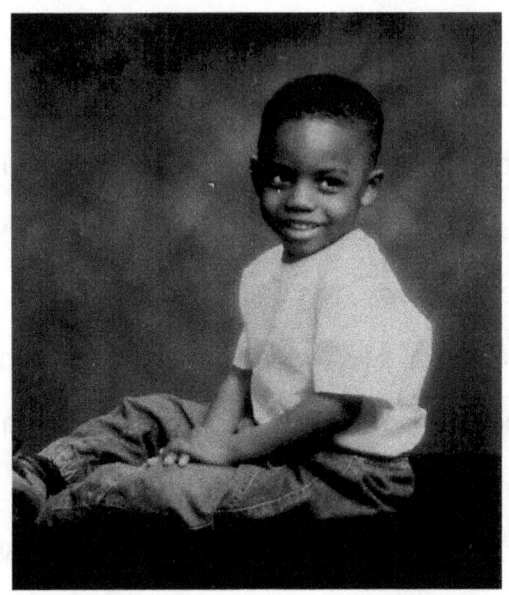

Robert at age 3

Robert was a good big brother for his sisters Raven and Rachel. He was very protective of his sisters. He loved them very much. He did everything that big brothers do to their younger siblings, including teasing them and playing practical jokes. Anytime they had problems and needed support, he was there for them. Robert was a joy to be around.

Misery to Motivation
By Riccardo L. Harris

Robert was artistic. He started drawing at an early age. Robert could draw anything that came to his mind. His drawings allowed him to draw the world as he saw it. What a gift.

Misery to Motivation
By Riccardo L. Harris

Robert's Artwork 2006

Misery to Motivation
By Riccardo L. Harris

2007

Misery to Motivation
By Riccardo L. Harris

Robert and his mother

Robert had a close relationship with his mother, Rosaland. They shared a special bond. He could talk to his mom about anything. She was there to listen and give him advice as needed. Robert was her only son.

Robert graduated from High School in 2006. After High School, Robert wanted to run track in college. He worked very hard during track season to earn an athletic scholarship. When Robert signed a letter of intent to run track at Ft. Scott Community College, I was a proud father. My son was going to college. Robert was graced with outstanding athletic ability. One of his friends that he worked out at the gym with came up to me after Robert's funeral service and said,

"Robert was the humblest person I knew. He was strong and athletic and he never rubbed it in anybody's face."

Robert signing a Letter of Intent to run track in college

After Robert's death, I heard many stories from his friends, family members and many others about how Robert affected their lives. He was only here for 19 years, but during his short lifetime he touched many lives. Robert's life was just beginning.

A few weeks before Robert's death, he told me about his excitement about the upcoming new year. He said,
"Dad, this next year is going to be my year. I just feel like something great is going to happen for me during this next year."

He was killed on January 5th, shortly after the new year started. I don't think that's what he had in mind when he said something great was going to happen.

Chapter 3
Failing as a Father

Becoming a father is one of my greatest accomplishments. It is something that I don't take lightly. I have always taken pride in being a good father. There are too many stories of fathers not being responsible in helping to raise and provide for their children. I chose to be the exception. I wanted to be the best dad that I could be.

I learned the lessons of fatherhood from one of the greatest men I have ever known, Alvin Holloway. Daddy Alvin, as he was affectionately called, married my mother when I was three years old. My brothers, Petey, Shaun and I were raised by this amazing man as if we were his own flesh and blood.

Societal rules would define Alvin Holloway as my step-father. That term limits what my dad was to me. The connotation attached to the word gives the impression that this person is someone who is less than the biological father. He was much more than that to me. He taught me how to ride a bike, how to throw a ball, how to catch, how to shoot a basketball. He taught me how to be a man and how to be a father. I just called him Daddy.

My dad always told us,

"If you lie, you will cheat. And if you cheat, you will steal."

According to my father, lying was one of the worst things someone could do. We used to get in more trouble for lying than misbehaving. He let us know that lying was disrespecting yourself and the person you are lying to. There were many lessons that my dad taught me. The major lessons he taught me dealt with being *respectful, being responsible and being resilient.*

While growing up, I never knew what kind of father I would become. I just knew that I wanted to be a good dad. I had a great example. I thank

God for sending me a Daddy to teach me how to be a man and how to be a good father.

A father's role is to provide for, to protect, and prepare his children for adulthood. Until January 5, 2008, I felt like I had done a fairly good job. When I was standing in the Emergency Room at the hospital waiting to hear about the well-being of my son, it dawned on me that I failed to protect him. I failed to keep him safe. I failed in my role as father. This was my internal struggle. Nobody knew what I was feeling. Nobody knew what I was going through. It was my pain and my guilt and that pain was very real to me.

How could I let something so horrific happen to my son? Thoughts of what he must have been thinking when it happened raced through my mind. Did he suffer? Was he scared? All of these questions stayed on my mind. To me, I failed in my role to protect my only son.

When Robert was 3 years old we had to rush him to the hospital emergency room. Robert had chronic asthma. Emergency room visits were a common part of our lives. During one particular visit, Robert was really struggling to breathe.

The nurse said, "Dad, can you hold him down while we give him a shot?"

They were giving him a shot to help with his breathing.

I approached my son very carefully. I really didn't want to hold him down, but I knew the shot would help his breathing. I didn't want him to experience the pain from the shot. As I held him down, his small frame was squirming in my arms. He looked up at me with tears in his eyes and said,

"Why are you letting them do this to me?"

I let him know that everything would be okay. He had to remain still so the nurse could help him to feel better.

I almost lost it. Tears started to well up in my eyes when I saw my little boy looking at me with fear in his eyes. I was supposed to protect him and in this case it appeared as if I was helping to cause him pain. I held him down long enough for the nurse to give him the shot. He continued to cry. The shot, along with the breathing treatments administered by the hospital staff, helped to improve Robert's breathing.

That experience has always been a vivid memory for me. I was trying to help, but to a three-year old, it appeared as if I was hurting him. Fast forward sixteen years later. Robert is lying on the bed in the hospital and doctors are doing what they can to try to save his life. I'm not present with my son in the hospital room this time. I'm not holding him down this time. I am anxiously waiting in the hospital waiting room to hear word on how he is doing. Feeling helpless, but prayerful that everything would be okay and my son would survive.

Parents want the very best for their children and they don't want them to suffer. When I think about how Robert died, it hurts me. It hurts because he experienced such a violent death. I was not prepared for this. No parent ever plans to bury their own child.

I do know that there was nothing that I could have done to prevent my son from being murdered. It still doesn't remove the pain associated with my wanting to protect him from violence. I did not realize that my own guilt was masking the fact that I was grieving.

The lessons that my dad taught me were passed on to my son; I was hoping he would pass them on to his children, but that didn't happen. He didn't have the opportunity to grow up, get married and have children of his own.

Chapter 4
God Why?

When I found out that my son was dead it really did something to my faith. It really rocked my faith to the core. I had so many questions. When Robert was killed, I had been in the ministry for 15 years. I thought that people who worked for God on a regular basis were immune to suffering, as if His people had a magical shield around them. This was not the case.

It took me a long time to realize it, but I was angry with God. I was very angry. I held that anger and frustration inside for a long time before I finally broke down and admitted it to myself. This is when my true healing began.

I had a belief that….with God all things are possible. I knew without a shadow of a doubt that He was with me and watching out for my family. Nobody could convince me otherwise. But when this event occurred…I was spiritually numb. I could not pray. No matter how much I tried, the words would not come out. I resorted to what I call popcorn prayers. These are prayers that are really quick like, "Lord, thank you for comforting my family during this difficult time." I knew he was there to comfort me, I just didn't know why he allowed this to happen to such a good young man.

I used to wake up early in the morning and spend time studying the bible and praying. That all changed after Robert's death. There was division in my relationship with God. I did not know it was there. My hurt was very strong. I felt like God let me down. He allowed my son to die. It took me a while to realize that I had distanced myself from God. I was getting on with my life, coping the best way I knew how.

Old folks used to say, "I thank God that I am in my right mind." I used to laugh at this, but there is a lot of wisdom in that statement. I can see how some people have mental breakdowns because of a traumatic experience. Although I was upset that God allowed this horrible event to occur, I realized that it was God who kept me sane through this entire process and for that I am truly thankful.

I'm wounded

Everybody grieves differently. Kübler-Ross has identified 5 stages of grief: denial, anger, bargaining, depression and acceptance. Although it appeared as if I was dealing with the acceptance stage, I did not immediately deal with my own feelings.

The hardest thing for me to deal with during Robert's death was looking at my family's pain. I go back to that night in the emergency room when the doctor called the family together and said, "We couldn't save him." I looked at my family. My wife's eyes expressed the deepest pain I have ever seen. I felt so helpless. I wanted to make the pain go away. I wanted to remove the pain from her eyes but I couldn't. No matter what I did or said made the pain leave her eyes. I was in pain, but seeing the pain in her eyes hurt me more than anything. She lost her first born, her only son.

I remember going home from the hospital at 3:00 in the morning. I sat down on the couch in total disbelief. I didn't sleep at all that night. I was trying to wrap my mind around the fact that my son was dead. Not only that, I was trying to understand why he was murdered. What did he do to deserve this? Who would do this to MY son?

My daughters, Raven and Rachel, were in pain as well. Raven was 15 and Rachel was 14 at the time of Robert's death. I felt like I had to hold everything together for everybody. Nobody put pressure on me to do this, I just felt like I had to be strong for them. The focus on their well-being was my way of not dealing with my own pain. I was hurting but trying to hide that hurt by staying busy. I thought I was caring for my family by not focusing on my pain. Actually I was hindering their healing as well as my own.

My pride would not allow me to deal with my own hurt and pain. I was so concerned about everybody else. I wanted to make sure they were okay, but on the inside I was boiling. This manifested itself in different ways. At times I would snap and say something out of character to someone for no reason at all. They could have been asking me how my day was going and I would respond in a very matter of fact manner. I was wounded and I didn't want anybody to know. To me this meant I was a failure.

My pride would not allow me to deal with my own hurt and pain.

My relationship with my wife was strained. Every time I looked at her, I saw the hurt and emptiness in her eyes and I felt helpless because I could not do anything to make that go away. That caused me to spend more and more time alone…alone with my own thoughts. This was not good.

Two years after Robert was killed, I reached my breaking point. All at once my emotions regarding Robert's death started to come out. I was angry and I didn't know why. During this difficult phase in my life, I pushed everybody away. I was hurting badly and I didn't know how to deal with that hurt. In the past I could call on God and He would help me to make it through. I felt like a man who was spinning numerous plates. One by one, the plates started falling and I felt like I could not control anything. The feeling of being out of control scared me. I needed to make sense of this.

I soon realized that my foundation was cracked. My relationship with God was not where it used to be. I had lost my way. During this time, I continued to work as a teacher and I continued in my role as the Pastor of a local church. I was leading, but I was bleeding. My journey to healing truly began once I reached that breaking point.

I had to get to the bottom of what was going on with me. I contacted a friend who is a therapist and he referred me to a therapist who would help me to begin to look at my pain. Looking back on the situation, I wish we would have sought counseling as a family. Each of us dealt with the loss differently. This would have allowed us to heal together.
Our family was fractured. Through the prayers of many and the support of our family and friends we made it through.

I was leading, but I was bleeding.

There is a wonderful story that describes what I went through. It is called Footprints by Carolyn Carty.

One night a man had a dream. He dreamed He was walking along the beach with the LORD. Across the sky

Misery to Motivation
By Riccardo L. Harris

flashed scenes from His life. For each scene He noticed two sets of footprints in the sand. One belonging to Him and the other to the LORD.

When the last scene of His life flashed before Him, he looked back at the footprints in the sand. He noticed that many times along the path of His life there was only one set of footprints. He also noticed that it happened at the very lowest and saddest times of His life.

This really bothered Him and He questioned the LORD about it. LORD you said that once I decided to follow you, you'd walk with me all the way. But I have noticed that during the most troublesome times in my life there is only one set of footprints. I don't understand why when I needed you most you would leave me.

The LORD replied, my precious, precious child, I Love you and I would never leave you! During your times of trial and suffering when you see only one set of footprints, it was then that I carried you.

As with the man in the story, God carried me during the most difficult time in my life. I felt like I was all alone, but looking back I realize it wasn't me. The faith that I thought had left me, was the very thing that was sustaining me.

Misery to Motivation
By Riccardo L. Harris

I love God with my whole heart and I realize that I never would have made it without Him being present in my life. The question of Why comes up in my mind from time to time, but I am okay because I know God loves Robert and He loves me too. God covered my family and carried us through the most difficult part of our lives. He is our foundation and I am very thankful for His love.

I know that I am not the only person to ever be mad at God. I'm glad that I realized it and came to terms with it. This helped in my healing.
I think about the story of the great singer Thomas Dorsey who is considered to be the Father of Gospel Music.

One night while Dorsey was leading a church service, a man came to the stage with a telegram for Dorsey. The telegram said that his wife had died giving birth to their child. Within 24 hours, the child died too. This sent Thomas Dorsey into a depression. He vowed to never write another hymn again. He doubted God's goodness. He shut himself in his house and didn't come out. After some time, he found himself singing from the depth of his soul. Out of his great pain came one of the most memorable gospel songs, *Precious Lord.*

Precious Lord, take my hand,
Lead me on, let me stand,
I am tired, I am weak, I am worn;
Through the storm, through the night,
Lead me on to the light:
Precious Lord, take my hand
lead me home.

Chapter 5

Forgiveness

To err is human, to forgive is divine.

-Alexander Pope

These words written by Alexander Pope in his *Essay on Criticism (1711)* have become somewhat of a cliché in many instances. All humans make mistakes. Some human mistakes impact us more than others. How people respond to the mistakes of others is the difficult part, and therein lies the dilemma. Is forgiveness only a divine act, or are humans capable of forgiving?

Merriam Webster dictionary defines *unforgiving* as: "having or making no allowance for error or weakness".

I believe that humans are capable of forgiving. I remember when I walked in the courtroom for the first time and I saw the young man who killed Robert, I was conflicted. A part of me was so angry because this boy was responsible for taking the life of my only son. But on the other hand, my heart went out to him. The conflicting emotions were difficult to reconcile. I didn't understand what was going on inside.

After a year of delays and continuances in court, the District Attorney's office called to let us know that they were negotiating a plea deal. They wanted to make sure that we were okay with it. This was good news because God knows I did not want to have my family subjected to more pain by going through a trial. The boy who killed Robert pleaded guilty to 2nd degree murder. We would come back to court in less than two months for the sentencing.

At the sentencing hearing, our family was given the opportunity to speak to the young man who took Robert's life. Before we spoke, he spoke to all of us. He said,

"I am sorry for what I have done. I have heard a lot of wonderful things about Robert and I know he was a good person. I just hope that I could live to be as good as he was. I'm sorry."

I'm sitting in the courtroom next to my wife and I am crying. He is admitting that he killed my son. I'm glad that this tragedy is starting to have closure. Four members of my family spoke to him in the courtroom that day, including me and my wife.

I lamented over what I was going to say to him. Would I be angry and yell at him? Would I be calm and say what was on my mind? These are the thoughts that went through my mind leading up to this day. I started by saying,

"What does a person say to the man responsible for killing his only son?"

I called him by his name and said,

"I forgive you for killing my son. I will not hold hatred and bitterness in my heart towards you."

The words kept on coming out. Finally, I thanked the judge and I took my seat. It was now time for sentencing. The judge sentenced him to 24 years and 5 months in prison. This was the maximum sentence he could have received for pleading guilty to 2nd degree murder based upon his previous offenses.

My family left the courtroom that day feeling relieved that this was finally over. We were very grateful to the Wichita Police Department and the District Attorney's office for making sure the young man was caught and prosecuted to the fullest extent of the law.

Fast forward two years after the sentencing hearing. I was visiting my brother in prison with my other family members. We needed an extra chair so I went over to another table to borrow a chair. At that table seated was the young man who killed Robert. He was visiting with his mother. I said hello and he did too. Flashing through my mind were the words I said to him in the courtroom about forgiveness. I asked myself did I really forgive him. After his visit was over he came over to our table. We shared a few words and I spoke with his mother.

That experience was indescribable. It was at that moment that I realized that I truly forgave him. How?
My upbringing and my faith in God made me the man that I am today. My mother is the kind of person who is able to see good in any situation. She has a positive outlook on life. Mama always sees the glass half full. I think she passed that to me. The faith that I have allows me to see people how He (God) sees them…through the eyes of love.

Forgiveness

After I speak to a group during a conference or a workshop, I answer questions from the audience. I was speaking at college and one of the students asked me a profound question. He said, "You said that you forgave the boy for killing your son, yet you also said you are glad he is in prison for committing the crime. How is that forgiveness?"

There are many definitions for the word forgiveness. When I talk about forgiveness it means,

> *To cease to feel resentment against.*

Forgiveness does not mean that the person who committed the crime should not be punished. It is possible to forgive the person without excusing what they did.
It does not mean that he and I will now be friends and hang out. Forgiveness is not about the person who is being forgiven....it is about the person with the offense.

The Carousel

Every amusement park I have ever gone to had a carousel. This ride wasn't like the roller coaster that had so many twists and turns and flips, nor the other rides in the amusement park that went really fast and made me nauseous. On the carousel I would see older couples sitting peacefully and smaller children with their parents enjoying a leisurely ride. The carousel was a safe place. I can remember riding on one of the beautifully carved horses pretending I was really riding a real horse. The carousel provided enjoyment, but it was safe, serene and non-threatening. As much as I enjoyed riding on the carousel, it never took me to a destination. I went around and around 360 degrees. No matter how many times I rode the ride, I always ended in the same place that I started. This was the safest ride in the amusement park, but it doesn't take you forward...

The same is true for those people who are dealing with not forgiving someone. No matter what they go through in life, they continue to go back to the same place. This makes things difficult because when we don't forgive, we keep that chapter open in our lives and we never move on.

There are many people who have been hurt and experienced pain. Whether it was from physical or sexual abuse, a hurt from a broken relationship, an accident, a violent crime, or some other reason, everybody experiences hurt and pain. Many times there are people associated with that hurt or pain. It can be difficult to move past the hurt and pain.

Getting off the Carousel (Moving Forward)

How do you forgive? I think it is different for everybody. For some people, the carousel continues to go around and around. They are stuck. They have been on that ride for years. Some of that could have something to do with not forgiving yourself. If we don't forgive ourselves for whatever part we think we played in our trauma, we will remain stuck.

There are people who are still stuck in 1985. They were hurt by someone and they never got over it. The person who hurt them has moved on. Forgiveness brings peace to the person who is suffering.

There are different schools of thought when it comes to forgiveness. Nobody is going to wave a magic wand and everything is going to be okay. There is work involved. There are no shortcuts. If you research forgiveness you will find many different programs and books about forgiveness. There is the 13 step approach, the 7 step approach, the 5 step approach and many others. I personally like what Mark O'Meara has to say about forgiveness in his book: *"The Feeling Soul - A Roadmap to Healing and Living"*. He says, "Admit you are angry; Acknowledge the loss and consequences; Submit to a feeling of vulnerability; Stop punishing; Identify some good in the other person; Develop genuine neutrality; and Stay in the present."

Personally, I decided that I was not going to be a victim any longer. This horrible tragedy changed our family forever. An innocent young man lost his life too soon. I chose to get off of the carousel and start moving forward.

Motivation

Chapter 6
The Character Challenge

I was determined to not allow my son's death to be in vain. In my mind, there had to be a purpose. I was sick and tired of turning on the news and hearing about young black boys killing each other. What could I do to change this? One person can only do so much. I had to tell Robert's story.

I have had the opportunity to speak at many schools, colleges and conferences across the country. During my presentations I talk about what happened to Robert. After I tell his story, I challenge the audience members to think about what I call the Character Challenge. This challenge is based upon agreeing to three different things; Be Respectful, Be Responsible, and Be Resilient. What is character? Character is: The mental and moral qualities distinctive to an individual.

I like the definition of character used by Ron Kurtus from the School for Champions. He says,

"Your character is based on the opinion of others, as well as your own view. When you have a reputation of having good character, people tend to treat you with respect, trust and admiration."

So our character speaks to what other people think about us. Ron Kurtus goes on to say that there are three character trait classifications: Personal, social, and group based character traits. Our personal character deals with our own motivation and how we respond to challenges. Our social character deals with our attitudes towards people. And our group character deals with how we follow rules.

When we die, what do we want people to remember about us? Do we want to be known for having the nicest clothes, shoes, or things? Or do we want people to remember how we treated other people? Our character speaks volumes.

Our family members and friends will definitely have nice things to say about our character, but what about others? What will they say about you?

Respect

According to police reports, my son was killed because the shooter felt like he looked at him the wrong way. In some way, he felt as if Robert had disrespected him. I hate this because we see this kind of story frequently on newscasts: Black on black violence. Black teenagers and young adults are dying every day because of this word respect.

What is respect? If you ask people to define this word, there will be many different answers. Which definitions are right? Respect from one's own perspective is very important. How we personally define this word determines how we treat ourselves and how we treat other people.

Misery to Motivation
By Riccardo L. Harris

I did a survey at the local high school where I taught math. The survey asked students one question: What is respect? Out of 1800 students, I received over 1000 responses. The responses to that one simple but profound question allowed me to see into the minds of teen aged boys and girls. Most of the responses were similar to the Golden Rule: Treat others like you want to be treated, but a few of the responses surprised me. One student wrote,

"Respect is not calling a girl the "B" word."
Another student wrote,
"Respect means everybody better stay out of my way."
Another wrote,
"Adults want us to respect them, but they don't respect us."

The subject of respect intrigues me. I often ask people what they think about the word 'Respect'. I ask friends, colleagues, mentors and anybody who will answer me. Most of them said the same basic things that the students said. One person emphatically said,

"Respect is earned!"

I tried to determine whether this person was speaking from the heart or whether they were repeating what they heard someone else say. I agree with that statement to a certain extent. Respect is earned if you give person a fair opportunity to show you who they really are. People make snap judgments every day based upon how they were raised and based upon their experiences. Those experiences can make people jump to conclusions based upon previous positive or negative experiences. We approach all life circumstances with our own biases. At times these biases get in the way when it comes to interacting with other people.

    I have heard people say, "I don't care if you don't like me, I just want to be respected." What they are really saying is, 'I want you to see me for

Misery to Motivation
By Riccardo L. Harris

who I am, and when you don't see me for who I am, I feel like I am invisible.'

"I am an invisible man. I am a man of substance, of flesh and bone, fiber and liquids - and I might even be said to possess a mind. I am invisible. Misunderstood, simply because people refuse to see me. When they approach me they see only my surroundings, themselves or figments of their imagination, indeed, everything and anything except me.

Ralph Ellison (1954)

It is a sad commentary when people feel like they are invisible. Often times this feeling of invisibility will cause people to do things so that they can be seen. We see students acting out in classrooms or being the class clown. They may not be stellar students, but they get attention one way or another.

"Black males today live in a world that pays them the most attention when they are violently acting out"

-bell hooks (2004)

Attention is attention; whether it is positive or negative.

When I talk about respect, I like to use this definition from goodcharacter.com.

Respect is valuing yourself, valuing others and valuing the world around you.

Are you a respectful person?

Answer these questions:

• Do I treat other people the way I want to be treated?

• Am I considerate of other people?

• Do I treat people with civility, courtesy, and dignity?

• Do I accept personal differences?

• Do I work to solve problems without violence?

• Do I never intentionally ridicule, embarrass, or hurt other people?

I know for a fact that when I was growing up, I was not a respectful person. As I said before, I talked about everybody. I was very mean. I was downright cruel to some people.

Responsibility

> Responsible people are accountable, pursue excellence, and exercise self-control.

Use your head; think before you act; imagine the consequences. Accepting responsibility is a vital part of maturing. When Robert was younger and he got in trouble for doing something wrong, he always blamed other people for what happened. If he got in trouble at school, he would blame the kid sitting next to him. If he got in trouble at home, he would blame his sisters. I realized that my son was maturing as a person when he began to accept responsibility for his own mistakes. One time when he was older, he got in trouble in school. I can remember asking him what happened and his response to me was,

"I messed up."

When my child who had blamed others for his misfortune and mistakes began to accept responsibility, I was amazed. I was at a loss for words. The angry dad turned into proud dad. I wasn't proud because he messed up. I was proud because he was growing into a responsible young man.

Sometimes people blame others for their mistakes. I have heard too many to list them all, but here are a few:
"I cannot get ahead in life because I am black."
"That teacher is racist."
"I didn't have enough time."
All of these excuses are used to shift the focus from the person with the problem. This mindset is common. Learning to be responsible can be a valuable character trait to develop.

Characteristics of a responsible people:
- They take care of their own business. They don't make others do what they are supposed to do.
- They take responsibility for their actions; and they don't make excuses or blame others.
- They are reliable and dependable; when they agree to do something, they do it.

Resilience

"The ultimate measure of a man is not where he stands in moments of comfort and convenience, but where he stands at times of challenge and controversy."
 -Martin Luther King Jr., Strength to Love, 1963

Dr. King's statement about the measure of a man speaks volumes. The very essence of who we are is truly revealed when we face our most difficult moments. I never thought about responding to a situation like this because it never crossed my mind. I never thought I would lose one of my children because they were murdered.

The character of a man is revealed when he faces difficult times. Who we are…is revealed during tough moments.

Resilience means to 'bounce back' when bad things happen. My family and I are bouncing back from this horrible tragedy that happened to Robert by sharing this message. Our recovery did not happen overnight. It is still a work in progress. Dr. King was right when he said that the measure of a man is revealed when he faces adversity. I will go even a step further. A person's true friends are revealed when he faces trials and adversity.

When Robert died, our family received such an outpouring of love and support from our community. The school where I worked, Southeast High School, wrapped their arms around our family during that difficult time. I also heard from friends that I haven't spoken to in over 20 years. One of my oldest friends called me from Iraq to let me know that he had heard the news and he was praying for us.

So resilience is not just about bouncing back on your own. It is about using all of your resources. This can include family, friends and community, or whoever is part of your support system.

Suspended from school

As a 9th grader in Junior High School I was very popular, at least I thought I was popular. I was the President of the Student Council, the captain of the basketball team and I was also the president of a group called Peer Leadership. This group went to other schools in the district to talk about the effects of using drugs and alcohol. I was good looking, cocky, arrogant and full of pride. I didn't realize it, but things were getting ready to change.

Misery to Motivation
By Riccardo L. Harris

One Friday afternoon at the end of the semester, the basketball team had a game. We lost the game by 30 points. On the way home from school after the game, my brother Shaun and I sat at the back of the bus. A friend had given me some marijuana a few days earlier, so I decided to fire it up. I wanted people to see how cool I really was. I was confident that no one would tell on me because I was "the man". I lit the marijuana and smoke filled the bus. After the people on the bus started laughing, the bus driver pulled the bus over. I put out the marijuana and placed it in the heating vent. The bus driver called for security. After a short investigation, they were unable to determine who had drugs on the bus. At that time, none of my peers told on me. The bus continued its route.

That entire weekend I could not rest. My little brother asked me what I was going to do. I didn't know. I worried about what was waiting for me when I returned to school. I knew it wasn't over.

Misery to Motivation
By Riccardo L. Harris

On Monday morning the Principal called me into his office and said, "I heard you were smoking weed on my bus."

I said, "It wasn't me".

He said, "I'm going to talk to every student that was on that bus to see if you are telling the truth."

I went back to my classroom and waited. Why didn't I just go ahead and tell him that I did it? At the age of 15 I had this mindset: If they have no proof, it didn't happen. Eventually he called me back to his office.

"I got you." He said. "I talked to several people who were on the bus and they all said it was you who was smoking weed on the bus."

I hung my head down and continued to listen.

"You are suspended from school for five days. You are no longer the president of the student council. You are no longer on the basketball team. And you are no longer part of

Misery to Motivation
By Riccardo L. Harris

Peer Leadership. Oh, and by the way, you cannot ride the bus again. Now, let's call your parents."

I was crushed. I thought I was "the man". I didn't think anybody would tell on me. I made a bad choice and I had to deal with the consequences. My parents were not happy at all. My punishment was extreme, but warranted. I deserved what I got. I didn't realize it at the time, but this experience changed my life.

My dad made an appointment for me to meet with a federal parole officer. Mr. H. was a Vietnam War veteran. I sat in his office and he told me about fighting in the Vietnam war. He also told me about his job as a parole officer. Mr. H. said,

"I hear that you are using drugs. Keep up that behavior and you will be seeing me on a regular basis. Not because your dad brings you in here, but because the court orders you to see me." He said, "Most of my clients started out just like you, smoking a little weed. They graduated from weed and started doing harder drugs. Eventually those drugs controlled their lives. Is that want you want?"

"No sir", I said.

Tears started to roll down my face and I could not say a word. He talked to me and let me know that this is not what I should be doing. I don't know if it was seeing the scars from the wounds he received in Vietnam that scared me or if it was Mr. H. saying that I was going to be addicted to drugs that scared me more. I just knew I did not like that experience. I needed to change.

Looking back now I know that incident changed me. From that moment on I was serious about school. Starting the next semester I changed. I made the honor roll for the first time. As a matter of fact, I was on the honor roll every semester after that. I was determined to do my very best.

The experience could have crushed me, but it humbled me. I was so busy trying to be "the man" and impress other people, that I lost my way. This bad situation happened to me because of the choice that I made. All choices, good or bad, have consequences. I developed resilience. I made a mistake, but that is what it was, 'a mistake'. I was not going to allow that bad experience to crush me. Even today, I am determined to not allow bad moments to determine my happiness, my success or my future.

Carrots, Eggs or Coffee

I love hearing stories that cause me to think about myself and how I am living my life. I once heard a story about Carrots, Eggs or Coffee. The story goes like this:

A young woman went to her mother and told her about her life and how things were so hard for her. She did not know how she was going to make it and wanted to give up. She was tired of fighting and struggling. It seemed as though when one problem was solved a new one arose.

Her mother took her to the kitchen. She filled three pots with water and placed each on a high fire. Soon the pots came to a boil. In the first, she placed carrots, in the second she placed eggs and the last she placed ground coffee beans. She let them sit and boil, without saying a word. In about twenty minutes she turned off the burners.

She fished the carrots out and placed them in a bowl. She pulled the eggs out and placed them in a bowl. Then she ladled the coffee out and placed it in a bowl. Turning to her daughter, she asked, "Tell me, what do you see?"

"Carrots, eggs, and coffee," replied her daughter.

The mother asked her daughter to feel the carrots, who did and noted that they were soft. The mother then asked her to take an egg and break it. After pulling off the shell, the young woman observed the hard-boiled egg. Finally, the mother asked her to sip the coffee. The daughter smiled as she tasted its rich aroma.

The daughter asked, "What does it mean, mother?"

Misery to Motivation
By Riccardo L. Harris

Her mother explained that each of these objects had faced the same adversity--boiling water--but each had reacted differently.

"Which are you?" the mother asked. "When adversity knocks on your door, how do you respond? Are you a carrot that seems strong, but with pain and adversity, wilts and become soft and loses strength? Are you the egg that appears not to change but whose heart is hardened? Or are you the coffee bean that changes the hot water, the very circumstance that brings the pain. When the water gets hot, it releases the fragrance and flavor. If you are like the bean, when things are at their worst, your very essence will change your environment for the better, making it sweet and palatable."

Author-Unknown

May we all desire to be like the coffee bean. No matter how tough things get, the coffee endures and changes its' environment. Which one are you?

The coffee bean in that illustration did not allow the painful situation (the boiling water) to mess up its destiny. Sometimes we allow the bad things that happen in our lives to mess up our future. We cannot allow our storms, trials, tragedies or disappointments to determine our future. When things get the toughest or the hottest, that should bring out the very best in us.

Your character is all you have. What do you want people to remember about you?

Chapter 7

A Dream Deferred

What happens to a dream deferred?

Does it dry up

like a raisin in the sun?

Or fester like a sore--

And then run?

Does it stink like rotten meat?

Or crust and sugar over--

like a syrupy sweet?

Maybe it just sags

like a heavy load.

Or does it explode?

-Langston Hughes

Each line in Langston Hughes' poem is a series of questions that causes the reader to consider individually and collectively. He begins by asking the question; what happens to a dream deferred? Each successive question is referring to the initial question. The first time I read this poem, I was 18 years old. I read anything and everything because I wanted to know myself. I was seeking an understanding of who I was. I call that my self-discovery phase. My impression of the poem then and my impression of the poem now are very different.

At the age of 18, I thought I could change the world. I was an intelligent young man with dreams of becoming a great attorney and making a difference. I was determined to not allow my dreams to be put off or go unrealized. Needless to say, I did not become an attorney, so that dream never came to pass, but I found another path. That path involved helping people. I have dedicated my life to helping young people.

My son had dreams that were never realized because he lost his life at the age of 19. He loved to draw. He had a gift. This boy was amazing. In the first grade he started drawing. I can remember him coming home from school one day and looking through his homework packet. He showed us the work he had done the previous week. He was asked to draw a tree in class. I was amazed when I looked at that tree. It didn't look like a first grader had drawn the picture. The tree was drawn with such detail. It looked like a real tree. It was at that moment that we realized that Robert was gifted in art.

Robert's Picture of Dad 2001 Age 13

His passion for drawing grew as he got older. Robert drew pictures of different types of things. He drew portraits of family members, super heroes and all types of animals. Just before he died, Robert was working on a new project. He decided to start his own clothing line. He was designing his own t-shirts and jeans. 2008 was the year he was launching the clothing line.

Picture drawn by Robert at age 15

Prisons and grave yards are full of people with unrealized dreams or dreams deferred. How

Misery to Motivation
By Riccardo L. Harris

do people respond when they cannot experience the success they pictured in their minds? What was Langston Hughes talking about when he asks the final question of his poem....Or does it explode?

I see explosions all through my own community. This is manifested through the violence seen in gang activity, alcoholism, drug abuse and domestic violence. What would cause a man, woman or child to point a gun at another human being and pull the trigger with the hope of killing that other person? This fundamental question is asked by every person who has lost someone because of a violent crime.

I will believe that there are a number of reasons for this violence: unrealized dreams, a lack of identity and self-hatred.

I see explosions all through my own community

Misery to Motivation
By Riccardo L. Harris

Unrealized Dreams

"Hold fast to dreams,
For if dreams die
Life is a broken-winged bird,
That cannot fly."

          Langston Hughes

Unrealized dreams can be a source of extreme frustration. I have conversations with people from time to time and I hear them talk about their greatest moments in their lives. I hear them say, "I could have been…if only…

I think we all reminisce of days gone by and missed opportunities. We fantasize about how much greater our lives would have been if things were different. There is something that exists in each and every one of us that makes us want to be great. All of us want our lives to mean something.

Misery to Motivation
By Riccardo L. Harris

Whether we are trying to be the next Michael Jordan or the next Dr. Ben Carson, we all have dreams.

It is difficult to deal with when our reality does not match what we envisioned or dreamed for our lives. Little by little, a part of the man with dreams of changing the world begins to die when he faces opposition and real life hits him in the face. That glimmer of hope and excitement that used to shine in his eyes slowly fades away. He finds new ways to cope with his meaningless reality and acknowledges that his life has meant nothing. The use of drugs and or alcohol temporarily allows the person to escape.

Dreaming can be exciting, but it can also be painful when those dreams are not realized. It is easier to look back and reminisce about the good old days, than to dream big about a tomorrow knowing that those dreams may never come to. We cannot stop dreaming. If we do, we are acknowledging that our best years are behind us.

Misery to Motivation
By Riccardo L. Harris

Everybody has dreams. When I ask young people what they want to be when they grow up, I get all types of answers. I want to be a doctor, a lawyer, a NBA or NFL player.
What dreams do you have? What do you want to become and what do you want to accomplish? What is your plan for experiencing that dream?

Lack of Identity

There are many people who have low self-esteem. One of the reasons I didn't like myself was because I didn't know who I was. I had no identity. My parents raised me to be strong and independent. They instilled a level of confidence in me, but I still lacked an identity.

What I saw on television was not a clear picture of who I was. I saw black men portrayed as ignorant, lazy and as criminals. This was perpetuated through television shows, media and the movies. The only time I heard about blacks in a positive light was when they were competing in sports.

It was time for me to find myself. I started to do research on my own to find out about me and my heritage. I went on an extensive journey of self-discovery. That is when my love of reading truly began. It was well worth it.

When people do not have an identity, they search for belonging. Some of our young people are finding their place of belonging in gangs. These gangs give them a sense of purpose and family.

Self-Hatred

There are many people who do not like themselves. When they look in the mirror they see something they despise. This is especially true with some of our young black men.

I think about the young man who looked at my son and decided to take his life. What did he see when he looked at Robert? Reports show that

Misery to Motivation
By Riccardo L. Harris

he had been smoking marijuana dipped in embalming fluid, taking ecstasy pills and drinking alcohol. In no way am I excusing his behavior by saying that being under the influence caused him to commit that crime. I know this is conjecture, but I believe he killed Robert because he hated himself. Our kids are killing each other because they lack an identity and they hate themselves. By killing someone that looks like themselves, it is like committing suicide without having to die.

Growing up can be difficult

When I was in Junior High School, I was the person who talked about everybody. I talked about a person if he was short, tall, fat, skinny, smart, or dumb. I found a reason to talk about everybody. I was very skilled at analyzing other people. I made some people feel really bad because I was cruel with my words.

Why did I talk about everybody? Why was I so critical of everybody else? I realized that my criticisms of others shifted the focus from my own weaknesses to the weakness of others. I was very insecure. I didn't want anybody to focus on any of my shortcomings, so I went on the offensive and talked about anybody I came in contact with.

There are many people who are insecure. They don't know who they are and they don't realize their worth. These people may or may not like themselves. I did not like myself so it was easy to insult others. When I put other people down, it made me feel better about myself…temporarily.

As I got older my Dad talked to me about my own insecurities. He let me know that I didn't like myself. In order to get me to like myself, he had me to add something to my daily routine. It involved staring at myself in the mirror and talking. I had to look at myself and say, "I like you." Not once or twice, but many times over.

This exercise made me sick. I thought it was stupid. I realized that I didn't like looking at myself in the mirror. It made me think of everything that I wasn't instead of focusing on what was right with me. I didn't like myself at all, but this exercise started me on the path of liking me.

As I got older, I enjoyed watching the NBC show Saturday Night Live. They had a skit called Daily Affirmation with Stuart Smalley. Al Franken played Stuart Smalley. This guy was focused on the positive and his own worth. At the end of his skit he would look in the mirror and say,

"Because I'm good enough, I'm smart enough, and doggonit, people like me!"

This was very similar to the exercise my Dad had me to do while looking in the mirror. I laughed every time I saw it because it reminded me of a period in my life when I didn't like myself.

Chapter 8
Dealing with Frustration

When I was about 14 years old my dad taught me a valuable lesson. I got my first job working as a cook at a fast food restaurant. I was excited about this new job. I found a used bicycle in the newspaper. I bought it so I could ride to and from work without needing a ride from my parents. I was growing up and trying to take responsibility.

After riding the bike for a week or so, the bike broke down. My brothers and I were good at taking bikes apart and putting them back together, so I thought I could easily fix the broken bicycle. I set up the bike out in front of the house and proceeded to work on it. For some reason, it was not cooperating with me at all. I got mad. I started cussing. I remember kicking the bike over because of my anger and throwing down the tools several times. I don't have to tell you about the choice language I used during this ordeal.

My dad, being the teacher of life lessons, came outside and said,
"Son, you are frustrated, why don't you take a break and go do something else. Come back to this project later."

There is a difference between taking a break for a while and quitting or giving up.

I told him I was going to try to work on it a little longer because I thought I could fix it. My dad understood something that I didn't at that time. He understood that when someone is frustrated, they don't have the ability to think and process things clearly. Their judgment is clouded because of the frustration.

Pride is something that plagues many people. Pride will not allow you to say I am frustrated. I was determined to get this bike fixed. I felt like if I took a break, I was admitting defeat. There is a difference between taking a break for a while and quitting or giving up.

I reluctantly took a break and started doing something else. Later on that evening I came back to the bike and fixed it in less than five minutes. My father could have told me what I was doing wrong. He could have even fixed the bike for me, but he saw an opportunity to teach me a better lesson.

Life is filled with disappointments and frustrations. If we allow the things that frustrate us to mess up our lives, those frustrations are victorious. But if we are willing to take a break and focus our attention some other place, we will realize that nothing is too hard to overcome. I fixed my bike, but I learned an invaluable lesson. Frustration can cause a person to have a limited view. Frustration often times leads to making decisions based upon desperation.

I can remember sharing the very same lesson with Robert. He was a lot like me. He wasn't going to give up easily. He could always find a way to get things done.

Know Your Limit

Every man, woman, boy or girl should know his or her limit. We all should know our breaking point…the point where we lose all control and make irrational decisions. I have come across many young people who do not know their limit. This hurts them because they don't know the triggers that may push them over the edge. Every person's trigger is different. If these triggers can be identified, the potential for an altercation or violence could be averted.

Some questions that may need to be explored are; what happened immediately before you lost control? And, is this a pattern? Does this happen on a regular basis?

Misery to Motivation
By Riccardo L. Harris

I talk a lot about the school setting because it is the setting that I am most familiar with. Students who have been labeled as incorrigible or un-teachable may have reached their breaking point a long time ago and every teacher or adult figure they come in contact with now is dealing with the effects of the fact that this student reached their limit a long time ago. It is sad when a child gives up on school because he or she feels like the world gave up on them a long time ago.

The challenge is to find out what motivates the student by building a relationship with him or her. This will show the student that you care.

The message of knowing your limit is not just for young people. It is a message that should speak to all of us. Sometimes adults get into power struggles with young people. These power struggles are meant to put the child in his or her place. To the adult, it gives the adult the upper hand, but to young person he or she may feel like adults really don't care. In power struggles, there always has to be a winner and a loser, but ultimately both parties lose. As adults, we have to make sure that we are not killing the spirit of our youth by what some may say is 'putting them in their place'. And young people need to understand that all adults are not against them.

Chapter 9
Dealing with the Scars

One of the worst accidents I have ever experienced happened one summer when I was a teenager. My brother Shaun, my cousin Kelly and I were riding our bikes home from the swimming pool. My duffel bag that contained my swimming trunks and towel was hanging from the handle bars of my bicycle. I quickly turned the corner and my duffel bag got caught in the spokes of the front wheel. I was thrown from the bike and my body slid along the asphalt on the street. I was hurt. I had scrapes and cuts all over my body. After dressing my wounds I took it easy for the next week or so. I was sore. Thankfully it was nothing serious.

When I look in the mirror today, I can still see the scars that are left over from that accident. The pain associated with those scars disappeared a long time ago, but the scars remain. We all experience different types of trauma in our lives. The trauma filled experiences produce scars. Some scars are physical in nature, but many scars are emotional scars. Scars are indicators that an injury has occurred.

When Robert died, I experienced an emotional heartbreak. The hurt from that wound was not visible; it was an internal hurt. To the outside world it may have looked as if everything was okay with me. I smiled, I laughed, but I still was dealing with the hurt and pain deep inside.

There are emotional scars that we get when we experience emotional heartbreaks. These scars are not like the scars that you can see on your skin, they are hidden deep inside of our hearts. Emotional wounds are the most difficult to recover from. With a natural wound, we are able to add antibiotic ointment and wrap it up and periodically check the progress. When it has healed, we take off the bandages and keep on moving.

With emotional wounds we cannot see if they are healing. There are no bandages to tend to and no ointment to apply. Some say that time heals all wounds. The passing of time does not always make the pain disappear. Internal walls are sometimes built to prevent us from feeling the hurt and pain. The realities of emotional wounds and scars are revealed when something or someone causes us to open our hearts and relive the trauma or tragedy.

If you are hurting seek help. There are many great counselors, therapists and pastors who are available to help people to address the emotional wounds. Support groups are another good resource for people. It allows them to see that they are not the only ones dealing with that issue.

Scars are indicators that an injury has occurred.

Hurting people hurt other people

"I have learned now that while those who speak about one's miseries usually hurt, those who keep silence hurt more." C.S. Lewis

If we don't get help with addressing our problems, it is possible for us to hurt other people. I talked about how cruel I was when I talked about other people. I know that I was lacking something within. I was hurting. We live in a society today where people are hurt by others every day. This perpetual cycle of hurt causes people to be verbally, physically and sexually abused. It causes domestic violence cases to occur on a regular basis. And it causes people to murder other people. People that inflict this kind of pain on others are oftentimes acting out of their pain.

Am I saying that the young man who killed my son was hurting? I believe so. I also think it was a combination of other things that caused him to take Robert's life. Many people have experienced some kind of hurt or tragedy in their lives. These tragedies do not give them an 'excuse' to do bad things to other people.

Conclusion

Death is difficult to deal with; especially when it happens to a loved one or someone close. As parents, we often imagine and anticipate the growth and future of our children. What will they become as adults? What will they accomplish in life? Will they go to college? As they pursue the American Dream, will most of their future fantasies become realities? Of all of the many things we imagine for our children, I don't believe that any parent ever visualizes burying a child – and neither did I. Losing my son was and still is the most miserable event I have ever encountered. Not only was I faced with dealing with the death of a child that I loved even more than I love myself; but I also felt helpless for not being able to prevent this tragedy from happening.

My entire family experienced extreme grief when Robert was killed. Going through the healing process was difficult. I do not wish that kind of pain on anyone. We were determined to not allow ourselves to stay in that state of Misery. Our hurt and pain motivated us and because of that motivation, we are better. Have we completely healed from this tragedy? No, I don't believe so, but we are much better than we were when the tragedy first occurred. Healing is an ongoing process.

For some people, seeking the help of a professional like a therapist or a counselor may appear to be a sign of weakness. It is not! It is a sign of strength. Acknowledging that you need the help of a professional or a support group is a way for you to take control of your life and start on a road to healing. Difficult situations will take place in our lives no matter what. It is up to us to determine whether these situations will make us bitter people or push us to become better people. The manner in which we respond to misery will determine whether or not it destroys our lives or motivates and empowers us to continue on the path to greatness.

What inspires us as individuals? It is obvious that our brightest moments are inspirational, but I have learned through this experience that inspiration can also exist in our darkest hours. The first time I held Robert in my arms, I instantly fell in love and became immediately inspired to become the best father I could be. My own father had provided wonderful examples pertaining to manhood and I was anxious to pass these same life lessons on to my son. Initially, his death left me feeling that both of us had been robbed. He had been robbed of the opportunity to experience so much of what life still had in store for him, and I had been robbed of the opportunity of experiencing his growth and maturity as a man. The very joy which had once inspired me to pursue excellence as a parent had been taken from me. I literally felt destroyed!

Never did I imagine this tragic situation ultimately inspiring me with a passion equally powerful to that which accompanied holding a living and breathing baby boy in my arms for the first time; helping him purchase his first car as a teenager; or seeing his infectious smile on countless occasions throughout the years. But in a unique way, I am just as inspired by the death of my son as I am by those special moments that represent his living. It is a different type of inspiration, but a very powerful inspiration nonetheless.

Young African American men are killing one another at an alarming rate, but senseless acts of violence impact young men and women of all nationalities. It is my desire to use the death of my son as a platform to teach character and values to young people of all ages and nationalities.

Teaching them *Respect* (to value themselves, value others and value the world around them); *Responsibility* (encourage them to be accountable, pursue excellence, and exercise self-control); and teaching them *Resilience* (to bounce back when bad things happen).

I hear stories about people saying that growing up without a father ruined their lives. Based on personal experience, I believe that fathers play an important role in the lives of their children, but there have been many people who have grown up without fathers and yet they have beat the odds and have lived rewarding lives. Some would say that they pulled themselves up by their own bootstraps. Personally, I don't think this is possible. Some people possess an internal fortitude that pushes them to succeed, but every highly successful person that I have met or read about has had someone helping them, inspiring them and guiding them. Perhaps it was a mother, father, grandparent, teacher, coach or someone else who took a special interest or belief in them. The so called 'self-made' man is a myth to me. Everyone needs guidance and support along the way even though some express a false sense of pride in boasting otherwise. Support does come in different forms, as does motivation. What motivates and inspires me may not have the same impact on the next person. This is a huge part of what makes each of us unique and special. I would be willing to go out on a limb and say that *Respect, Responsibility and Resilience* are at the core of what has motivated just about all success stories. Successful parents, successful students, successful business people and success in all facets of life are heavily predicated on these three values.

    I am on a mission to put all of my blood, sweat and tears into ensuring that my son's legacy is one that shines just as brightly as his beautiful smile and warm personality. At times, I still feel a great deal of pain, misery and even anger; but those emotions are shifting into a passion to reach others in hopes of preventing other families from experiencing similar tragedy. I am on a personal crusade to ensure that Robert P. Ridge did not lose his life in vain, even if that means just making a positive impact on one young person; one father; one family.

Notes

Chapter 1
Wichita Eagle Newspaper Headlines January 8, 2008, January 9, 2008

Wichita Eagle Newspaper, Crowson's View January 9, 2008

Chapter 2
Sparks, Nicholas *The Rescue* (2001)

Chapter 4
Kübler-Ross, E. (1969) On Death and Dying, Routledge,

Footpritns by Carolyn Carty

Precious Lord song by Thomas Dorsey

Chapter 5
Pope, Alexander *Essay on Criticism* (1711)

Omeara, Mark *The Feeling Soul: A Roadmap to Healing and Living* (2005)

Chapter 6
Ron Kurtus, The School of Champions

King Jr, Martin Luther, *Strength to Love*, 1963

bell-hooks *We Real Cool: Black Men and Masculinity* (2004)

Chapter 7
A Dream Deferred and Dreams

The Collected Poems of Langston Hughes

Langston Hughes (Author)

Chapter 9
Quote by C.S. Lewis

Misery to Motivation
By Riccardo L. Harris

The Robert P. Ridge Foundation was established to bring awareness to others about the effects of gang violence. For more information visit the website at www.rpridgefoundation.com.

Mr. Harris is available to speak at conferences, workshops, school events etc. For more information, please visit: www.rpridgefoundation.com.

www.ingramcontent.com/pod-product-compliance
Lightning Source LLC
Chambersburg PA
CBHW061454040426
42450CB00007B/1353